SNOOPY

(features as)

The Winter Wonder Dog

Charles M. Schulz

ℛℛ

PEANUTS is a registered trademark of
United Feature Syndicate, Inc.
Based on the PEANUTS® comic strip
by Charles M. Schulz.

Originally published in 1988 as 'Snoopy Stars as the
Terror of the Ice'.
This edition published in 2002 by Ravette Publishing.
Reprinted in 2007.

Printed in the UK by CPI Bookmarque, Croydon
for Ravette Publishing Limited,
Unit 3, Tristar Centre,
Star Road, Partridge Green,
West Sussex RH13 8RA

ISBN: 978-1-84161-288-1

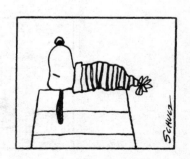

MARCIE, CHUCK'S LOST IN THE WOODS..HE NEEDS US TO FIND HIM...

GET YOUR BACKPACK... BRING ALL THE THINGS YOU NEED IN THE WOODS! WE'RE A RESCUE TEAM!!

I HAVE EVERYTHING, SIR.. FOOD, WATER AND COMIC BOOKS...

IT MAY BE A LONG TRIP...BRING AN EXTRA COMIC BOOK!

11-7

AS LONG AS WE'RE JUST PRACTICING, I HAVE A SUGGESTION

MAYBE YOU SHOULD SHOOT AT THE OTHER GOAL FOR A WHILE...

12-27

1-25   © 1983 United Feature Syndicate, Inc.

Other PEANUTS titles published by Ravette ...

Pocket Books

	ISBN	Price
Man's Best Friend	978-1-84161-066-5	£2.99
Master of the Fairways	978-1-84161-067-2	£2.99
The Fearless Leader	978-1-84161-104-4	£2.99
The Legal Beagle	978-1-84161-065-8	£2.99
The Master Chef	978-1-84161-107-5	£2.99
The Music Lover	978-1-84161-106-8	£2.99
The Sportsman	978-1-84161-105-1	£2.99
The Tennis Ace	978-1-84161-162-4	£2.99

2-in-1 Collections

	ISBN	Price
Book 1	978-1-84161-177-8	£4.99
Book 2	978-1-84161-178-5	£4.99
Book 3	978-1-84161-196-9	£4.99
Book 4	978-1-84161-197-6	£4.99
Book 5	978-1-84161-234-8	£4.99
Book 6	978-1-84161-235-5	£4.99
Book 7	978-1-84161-260-7	£4.99
Book 8	978-1-84161-261-4	£4.99

Little Books

	ISBN	Price
Charlie Brown - Friendship	978-1-84161-156-3	£2.99
Charlie Brown - Wisdom	978-1-84161-099-3	£2.50
Educating Peanuts	978-1-84161-158-7	£2.50
Lucy - Advice	978-1-84161-101-3	£2.50
Peppermint Patty - Blunders	978-1-84161-102-0	£2.50
Snoopy - Laughter	978-1-84161-100-6	£2.50
Snoopy - Style	978-1-84161-155-6	£2.50

Colour Collections

	ISBN	Price
The Many Faces of Snoopy (new)	978-1-84161-280-5	£19.99
It Goes Without Saying (new)	978-1-84161-272-0	£10.99
It Was A Dark & Stormy Night Snoopy	978-1-84161-245-4	£10.99
The World According to Lucy	978-1-84161-230-0	£9.99
It's A Big World Charlie Brown	978-1-84161-188-4	£9.99
It's A Dog's Life, Snoopy	978-1-84161-179-2	£9.99

Gift Books (hardback)	ISBN	Price
A Friend is forever	978-1-84161-213-3	£4.99
Best Friends understand sharing	978-1-84161-258-4	£4.99
Happiness is a warm puppy	978-1-84161-211-9	£4.99
Love is walking hand in hand	978-1-84161-212-6	£4.99
Peanuts Guide to Life Book 1	978-1-84161-268-3	£4.99
Peanuts Guide to Life Book 2	978-1-84161-269-0	£4.99
Peanuts Guide to Life Book 3	978-1-84161-287-4	£4.99
Security is a thumb and a blanket	978-1-84161-210-2	£4.99
True Love is complete trust	978-1-84161-259-1	£4.99
Black & White Landscapes		
Now, That's Profound, Charlie Brown	978-1-84161-181-5	£4.50
I Told You So, You Blockhead	978-1-84161-182-2	£4.50
Miscellaneous		
It's Your First Crush Charlie Brown (new)	978-1-84161-295-9	£7.99
Why, Charlie Brown, Why?	978-1-84161-231-7	£6.99
Peanuts Treasury	978-1-84161-043-6	£9.99

All Peanuts books are available at your local bookshop or from the publisher at the address below.

Just send your order with your payment and name and address details to: Ravette Publishing, Unit 3, Tristar Centre, Star Road, Partridge Green, West Sussex RH13 8RA.
(tel: 01403 711443 ... email: ravettepub@aol.com)

Prices and availability are subject to change without notice.

Please enclose a cheque or postal order made payable to Ravette Publishing to the value of the cover price of the book/s and allow the following for UK postage and packing:-

70p for the first book + 40p for each additional book
except:- *Peanuts Treasury* ... when please add £3.00 per copy
          Colour Collections ... when please add £2.50 per copy